MOMENTS

For ISMS, with whom the Son Shines

PUBLISHER

ParaBela's Bee, LLC
PO Box 770689
Memphis, Tennessee 38177

Print On Demand Version
ISBN 10 digit: 0-9905495-1-8
ISBN 13 digit: 978-0-9905495-1-2

Also Available – Electronic Version
ISBM 10 digit: 0-9905495-0-X
ISBN 13 digit: 978-0-9905495-0-5

FOR THE LOVE OF & FROM MOTHER,

Dedicated to my fathers,

Robert Samuel, who not only taught me the meaning
of love, but showed me, and;
Milo Patrick, who gave me many of my very best traits
…and worst.

And The Catholic Church, which very much guided
my faith and my formation, I am eternally thankful
and committed. And while knowing the limitation
within humanity, the Holy Spirit has no such limits
and continues to be ever present.

To the Lord's Divine Mercy; I trust in Our Lord.

To the Sacred Heart of Jesus and
The Immaculate Heart of Mary,
Bless the Papacy of Francis

*"In all truth I tell you, unless a wheat grain falls into the earth and dies, it remains
only a single grain; but if it dies it yields a rich harvest." John 12:24*

"Religion is a realization, not talk, not doctrines, nor theories;
however beautiful all they may be.
Religion is being and becoming, not hearing or acknowledging.
It is not an intellectual asset;
but the transformation of one's whole life."
Swami Vivekananda, known in his pre-monastic life as **Narendranath Datta**

Table of Contents

Introduction

I first began writing poetry around the age of sixteen. From then until the age of eighteen, I probably completed six to eight poems and then stopped writing. Although I had never really given it any thought, I considered all these early poems lost to time. Several years ago, after I had begun writing poetry again, my youngest sister sent me a letter that included a poem I had written in 1978. She found it in one of my mother's treasure boxes; seemed my mother found a copy of one of my poems and put it away for posterity unbeknown to me.

The written Word, Poetry has always been part of my heart, although I had not previously been that inclined to pursue writing more of it personally. At some point in my life, this changed and I am eternally thankful for all the events which lead to this change and the possibilities ahead.

I have long enjoyed exploring the Word of poetry; one of my favorite poems still, from childhood is Joyce Kilmer's "Trees." Another longtime favorite is Edwin Markham's "Outwitted." I enjoy its pure simplicity along with its outright insightfulness. Recently, I have taken a liking and study to the Brazilian poet, Mario Quintana.

It is my hope and wish you may find my poetry enjoyable and meaningful. One small note I have always found interesting; for whatever reason, I always begin writing a poem by first giving it a title.

Some of the proceeds from the sale of this work will be used for our charity projects within Brazil. Bringing clean, free water to people and communities in Northern Minas Gerais who are without, renewable energy – solar and wind - to people and communities throughout Minas Gerais, and energy efficient LED lighting to all of Brazil.

With peace and prayers,
Stephen Michael

Moments

What dictates measures of our time
Be it a watch, clock, even hourglass
In a world filled with so many signs
Our lives bound by future and past

While surely time exists for us not
Only here and now in all its glory
A hard reality, an unrelenting truth
Some might perceive an interesting story

Proper consideration to be given by all
Hopefully engraved in the mental sack
Life endlessly steps forward and then a fall
Time considers us not, preferring only smiling back

Shall gauging be the minutes, days, or years rasp
The record and timeliness of our journey
Or best captured in the moments we grasp
Of grace, beauty, happiness, His glory

So I depart with a toast, from me to you
Mostly best wishes for all God's Blessings
And little time pieces for each of you,
Hello, greetings, a guy named Stephen Michael

Let Me Tell You Of

Once introduced to new Brazilian spirit
Lovelier than a picture from inside out
Tall young slender and oh very smart
Aware mature was their nature no doubt

Strange may it seem always perceived most
The wise reflective elderly eastern sage
Though it really didn't suit well proper toast
As she signed Flavia name on life's page

Born from Minas fittingly perceived Beloish
Quiet unrevealing far reaching reserved thinker
Perhaps more accurately conceive Kathmanduish
Much more than words from this simple tinkerer

She focuses work constantly on multiple piles
Life school family work keeping world sane
Her heart mind pondering being named Kyle
Where it stands possibilities not getting maimed

No worries little doubt Flavia figures it all out
Correctly in time space certainly graceful class
Her spirit and person hard not to openly flout
And often I pray Kyle unravels her total mass

Wonder she'll ever know or fully comprehend
Much she's done and meant with someone afar
Who thinks world of her with wishes to send
Realizing all dreams in worlds fabulous bazaar

So I depart your day many thanks and hugs
Wishing one day soon raising toasting Jeroboam
Questing still with gift known as flats or plugs
For now hope T is satisfied with heartfelt poem

Izabela's Bee

Friends shout Bela about, birthday girl turning twenty four
Easy to perceive a tendering care, so much sensitivity
A world filled with life and needs, on hand to bore
Although Saturday please cherish and adore, celebrate with me

As birthday girl, most graciously securing twenty four
Hug and kiss bring me laughs, present a gift of yourself that lasts
Forever the smile, tranquil dose of whelming charm
Altogether we shall span, bridge concluding future and past

Cuz this weekend birthday girl, can you believe twenty four
Sharing my spirit allow please, achieving reach of zenith love
Person worthy such exalted affection, an angelic musical score
Could entity possibly exists, being comprised lion lamb mostly dove

Have you heard birthday girl, embracing twenty four
Takes me places and realms never been, completing journey as one
Fulfilling him things previously, hidden not completely understood
One author professes such love, I shall wait to see under the sun

Restoring to poets track, birthday girl now packing twenty four
Celebrate have some fun, gently forfeiting trepidation to others
After party said and done, the exiting will focus work ahead
Laboring resolve altogether, easing difficulties for sisters and brothers

Although now and evermore, birthday girl all of twenty four
If you happen upon me, I'll always accept your presence
The Spirit come unto us, Blessed be everyone's journey forward
Yearning life and love being within, receptive with universal essence

Izabela as stated, an ancient title purporting God's promise
A lady child, woman friend, sister daughter, a baby mother
So once again departing joyous toast, from me to you always
A guy that acts with hope, making presence conveying his druthers
Celebrating Bela heart and soul, a maestro Lady engaging vinte e quarto

My the Humanity

Who would have known, just a person I met sweating
A gentle lovely being, motioning through her many cycles
Hello how you doing, an austere smile always the setting
All the while a being, her focus temporarily only Michael

My what a gift she is, for me and all the world to see
A being seems I, not fortunate to have better known
Although today came to, appreciate with highest degree
Her being love integrity, internal peace appealing cologne

One being making a difference, it's comforting for sure
She'll help you out or take you down, impartial with status
My to honor protect serve, My what a lady indeed pure
Good having first hand knowledge, especially that it's gratis

My we wish all the best, advancing realm of God's essence
Our peace and prayers with you, confident of His Blessings
Easy to see why earthly beings, are praising your presence
Superb example to follow, My the humanity and caressing

In My humanity, there is divinity for all to observe

A Year of This World

Been nearly year since, sitting across speaking true profession
During all this time, my feelings affections only grow
For spirit being whom I've known, before time my confession
My thoughts and love endure, stirring always in my being to sow

A Lady's heart mind soul, beyond human comprehension to bow
A wondrous spirit who, wonders herself of this physical world
Finding solace support from, the creator comforter we all know
She advances in understanding, knowledge unfolds soon pearled

Has it been a year or nearly, seems to me more like eternity
Although required reflection, manifestations entire comprehension
Grasping welcoming life's real calling, a universe of heavenly serenity
Present in beyond this world, realizing now past four dimensions

Nice being easy albeit isn't the case, nor can it be absent some fight
For in trial and tribulation, purifies the heart mind and soul
As quoted in past, "what we obtain too easily, we esteem to lightly
tis dearest that gives everything its value" must trace to some ancient scroll

Though time has passed, please aware discern part of complete journey
For much shall pass very soon, with it grace happiness so much beauty
Believe this is true for I tell you so, as come to life off the gurney
While within my soul, also culmination of you past year trips to Haiti

This I know

I know a girl so special and sweet,
for me pronouncing just her name is more than a treat

A charm and allure so very great,
you'd consider jumping off a bridge the request of a saint

Her face so gorgeous and hip,
you kind of feel sorry for that girl launching only a 1000 ships

A profile more gorgeous and above par,
than beauty and light at night of 100 billion stars

The roundness so perfect an awe,
that with simple smile will come exact squaring of her jaw

A smile so lovely and bright,
only its radiance surely can approach glory of heavenly light

Her eyes and brow so magnificent,
just being in vicinity for a glimpse bestows beneficence

And her beautiful hair,
so fine and abundant no words better define meaning of flair

Her shoulders and neck couldn't be finer,
master artists desire to chisel them into rock and granite

Small hands so gentle and soft cover,
you'll feel comfortable and confident baby child friend or lover

Her arms chest waist and hips I can only mumble,
lest I get myself into some really big trouble

Except exists not form or figure to say,
I'd rather someday take horse cart ride filled with hay

Prior to this perhaps a chance at bliss,
caressing her calf ankle and big toe with sweet kiss

This I know and long before any of this,
seeing a girl, mostly making her laugh and sharing chats

Smile Which Erupts

When do you know you've really caught somebody's laugh
Shame on you if you've not heard a few of this one
Certainly pray more come this way and upon my behalf
Cuz I've heard the taste of some from earths only woman

Recall hearing her giggling a spell on several occasions
Though impossible for her delivering a snicker or cackle
She's much too righteous and noble thinking these situations
My goals and aspirations are among the giggles to be tackled

Although I've endeared several her sweet gentle chuckles
You'll never perceive tones of her snorting or braying
The Lady would never consider it once or ever buckle
Faithful to receiving more chuckles emerging thru her smiling

Think even once almost twice looming laughs from her belly
And truly I desire presence most any future ones forth coming
With many prayer wishes the day let her hair down with folly
For my dreams and joys realized heeding her belly fully roaring

My Broken Heart

What a joy to truly fully understand, a broken heart
A comprehension never experienced, before this life
Lucky maybe, or never had cause to expose my heart
Although yesterday, had the unique pleasure this strife

Sadistic you say, I must assure you really not the case
As for the remainder of my life, I shall be forever aware
All the risks involved with others loved, mostly with one
Knowing the hurt pain, any sane being never consider further

Shall We Make Our Future

Do we really understand the wastefulness we all create
Pulling and pushing on our mother which we call earth
Having total disregard for ourselves and children's fate
As earth's humans seem to push forever toward dearth

Little conscience only squandering resources day and day
Earth wishes this zeal might better focus with realizing love
For the preciousness and sacredness of our family's bouquet
And enjoying clear sunrise splendor watching morning doves

Shall we make our future creating like something of our past
Anicent understanding knowledge and love of Mother Earth
Recycling using less thinking ahead that it may last and last
Our hopes joys and happiness paving the way for the future births

"What Befalls The Earth, Befalls All The
Sons And Daughters Of The Earth"
Native American Saying

Our Sister's, My Sister's

We all have wondrous sister name Drita
Calling similar and devoted love of Jesus
Whose love envelopes us like warm pita
We should use sisters for doctoral thesis

While certainly divine they are only human
This particular one held only a short time
Although their light cast by a great lumen
Can't stopped spread of God's light divine

We keep our sister's with mind and prayer
Seeing the blue strip and flowing long white
Selfishly knowing reverse more true aware
Jesus', Mary's heavenly light coming in sight

Missionaries of Charity Sisters beings of grace
Throughout the world human race their place

I Have Come To Climb A Tree

I have come to climb a tree
and secure my breath of life
for the time has come to take place
I offer no resistance only peace

I have come to surrender my life
born of Spirit, Water, Heavenly light
returning only love, joy, harmony
My fullness being in plain sight

I come to lose all this world
its existence empty yet complete
arriving Belo this certain day
Oh Lord Master my Brother true

Oh hear me too sweet Mother
once again I call upon thee
for Wisdom, Truth and your Grace
I come this day to find my life

A Sunday Evening

Here sitting at Isabela's, pondering the self or lacking
Her pupils resting on springs, listening languages abound
Bookshelves filled with wisdom, diversion love stories backing
Speaker on screen reflects for, Isabela brings common sound

Who are these people asking myself, mixture clearly evident
What do they seek here, profoundness knowledge themselves
If they only dig down deeper, reach at last true sentiment
For this day they'll understand oneness, and claim their heavens

A Creature

They have long been great love of my life
A creature specifically chosen by our Lord
Endowed with spirit life similar ways of wife
Unfortunately man has long twisted for sword

Oh I recall so many experiences thrills calmness
Gentle walk lope movement filled trot or gallop
Whatever the time moment never any balminess
As I drift and ride through humanity's stirrups

A creature of respect so faithful true an oneness
Existence is and can only wisdom attributed too
A women's spirit love filled idea of blessedness
Whose imaginative love to overcome man's blue

How not we see beyond it this existence called matter
Our journey being long filled with much up and downs
Try conquering what does not really exist only scattered
Can only ponder this act looking back forward abound

A Poem To "Kid Knees"

Take care yourself, much needed
Clean my system, precious blood
Rid me of impurities, health seeded
Fail me not, organ much loved

Are we doing, all we could or should
Care for guard, one primary organ
The people in room, dedicated to good
Lest we lose, one of our orchids

View One (Vu1) of The World

I ask you how we've all become ensnared
Of both waves particles traveling via the air

By very first creation sent forth by universe
Essence of our very life becoming so perverse

How we so compromised ourselves and earth
Demands attention immediately and our rebirth

Rid our homes workplaces sacred spaces CFL's
The hideous light dangerous toxin is now no cell

Reclaim our earth and soul toward final light
Walk with us now joining end of insane blight

For either you can exist creatively mercury free
Or just continue buying free mercury not to bee

View One technology may not stop world hunger
Although promises assisting rid one great danger

Song

True Calling

When shall we arrive at the
time and place of our own choosing
When shall we deliver now or then
upon each of our souls true calling

Do we see others beyond ourselves
great suffering in such simple needs
Do we taste people's fear in our being
as we mouth about their silent crying

When shall our hearts turn from stone
into love made from hearts sturdy as rocks

Do we feel all the world is dying
as we live our lives in such isolation
Do we hear the calls of all the many
that their cries become drowned out

When shall our hearts turn from stone
into love made from hearts sturdy as rocks

Great release of God's Spirit in process
happening here..now..even greater ahead
Shall we harness it of our own choosing
magnifying his spirit more then six billion times

Satisfying shall God's promises bee, and
then shall our hearts turn from stone
into love made from hearts sturdy as rocks

Song
The Heart Of It

Where is this thing called a heart
is it really just pumping inside you
Vital organ muscling our lives away or
some vulnerable place that's inside us

Where is this thing called a heart
does it really just exist alone or is
It part of something truly much larger
a universal spirit beyond physical world

When shall we become the heart of it and
transform ourselves beyond into this world

Where is this thing called a heart
containing precious blood of human race
Supplying all the arteries and veins for
the sacred vessels of our earthly beings

Where is this thing called a heart
very small piece of part everyone's God
Who wishes we would do our destined part
performing works toward grace and peace

When will we become the heart of it and
transform ourselves beyond into this world

Where is this thing called a heart
creating a journey destination called love
And achieving peace that is but one grace
that we may find..know..fulfill our lives

When will we become the heart of it and
transform ourselves beyond into this world
Shall it be now or then…………..when

www.ingramcontent.com/pod-product-compliance
Lightning Source LLC
Chambersburg PA
CBHW080553030426
42337CB00024B/4867